What a

Elle.

Illustrated by Wendy Rasmussen

A Harcourt Achieve Imprint

www.Rigby.com
1-800-531-5015

The baby can eat.

The cat can eat, too!

The baby can drink.

The cat can drink, too!

The baby can smile.

The cat can smile, too!

The baby can crawl.

The cat can crawl, too!

The baby can walk.

The cat can walk, too!

The baby can play.

The cat can play, too!

The baby can cry!

But the cat can purr.